Praise for Messy F
Life Lessons from Imperfect

Jennifer has a unique gift of making the Bible applicable to living a victorious life in everyday situations! This Bible study encourages, convicts, and equips us as we seek Jesus in all that we do.
— **Judy C. Graham**, President and Co-Founder, Celebration Women's Ministry, Inc.

If you've ever felt like your life is a mess, this study is for you. Jen is a down-to-earth, in-the-trenches, authentic follower of Christ who guides with humor and practical insights as to how we can allow God to turn our messes into His masterpieces. You will love the life application this study brings, freeing us up from the "chains" culture pushes us into.
— **Steve Gladen**, Pastor of Small Groups, Saddleback Church and author of
Leading Small Groups with Purpose

I have seen Jen's life and ministry up close and can say with confidence that her heart is for seeing messy lives get whole and healthy. Messy People is about finding hope, balance, peace, and wisdom by being immersed in the lessons of Scripture. Thanks, Jen, for pointing us back to the source of peace in the midst of a messy world.
— **Carolyn Moore**, Founding and Lead Pastor of Mosaic United Methodist Church
in Evans, Georgia, and author of The 19: Questions to Kindle a
Wesleyan Spirit

Using the Bible, humor, probing questions, and her own life experiences, Jennifer helps you break through the clutter and confusion of life to uncover your destiny and identity in Christ. You will discover the God who delights in making a masterpiece out of your mess.
— **Jorge Acevedo**, Lead Pastor of Grace Church, a multi-site United Methodist
congregation in Southwest Florida

By the power of story you will be escorted through the messy lives of biblical people, and in the process you'll discover something of yourself. Fueled by insightful commentary, real life experience, and "I get it" humor, you will be delightfully reminded that God "did, does, and will" use messy people.
— **Shane Bishop**, Senior Pastor of Christ Church in Fairview Heights, Illinois,
and recipient of The Foundation for Evangelism's Distinguished
Evangelist Award

PEOPLE

LIFE LESSONS *from* IMPERFECT
BIBLICAL HEROES

a Bible Study by

JENNIFER COWART

Jenny Youngman, Contributor

ABINGDON WOMEN / NASHVILLE

Messy People
Life Lessons from Imperfect Biblical Heroes
Leader Guide

ISBN 978-1-5018-6314-1

18 19 20 21 22 23 24 25 26 27—10 9 8 7 6 5 4 3 2 1

Contents

About the Author

Jennifer Cowart is the Executive Pastor at Harvest Church, a United Methodist congregation in Warner Robins, Georgia, that she and her husband, Jim, began in 2001. Today Harvest serves about 2,500 people in seven worship services weekly. With degrees in Christian education, counseling, and business, she oversees a wide variety of ministries and enjoys doing life and ministry with others. As a gifted Bible teacher and speaker, Jen brings biblical truth to life through humor, authenticity, and everyday application. She and Jim have co-written several small group studies together, including *Hand Me Downs* and *Living the Five*. They are the proud parents of two children, Alyssa and Josh.

Follow Jen:

📘 Jim-Jennifer Cowart

📷 JimandJennifer Cowart

Website: jennifercowart.org / jimandjennifercowart.org
        (check here for event dates and booking information)

Introduction

Every life gets messy at times. Mine does, and surely yours does as well. Sometimes these messes are literal, like a house that would be easier to condemn than to clean or a child who needs a firehose instead of a tub. But sometimes our messes are harder to see. These intangible messes often have labels such as illness, conflict, depression, abuse, bankruptcy, divorce, and job loss. And often these messes are painful.

During this six-week study, we are going to dig into the lives of biblical heroes who were messy people too. Throughout the Scriptures we find wonderful but messy people God used in powerful ways. Together over these six weeks we will learn from the lives of Rahab, the prodigal son, Josiah, Mary, David, and Daniel. From their stories we will learn how God chooses to use broken people and how He restores damaged relationships. Through their examples we will see how God gives us power to handle our critics and deal with the hard moments of life. Along the way we'll discover that we don't have to just endure messy lives but can actually learn to thrive with God's guidance and help.

About the Participant Workbook

Before the first session, you will want to distribute copies of the participant workbook to the members of your group. Be sure to communicate that they are to complete the first week of readings *before* your first group session. For each week there are five devotional lessons that include both Scripture study as well as reflection and prayer. The lessons are designed to lead women through a quiet time with God where they savor His Word and allow Him to speak to them.

Encourage the women in your group to find a quiet place—maybe a favorite chair or a spot on the porch, weather permitting—where they can spend their devotional study time.

Each day the lesson follows the same format: Settle, Focus, Reflect, and Pray. On average the lessons can be completed in about twenty to thirty minutes—depending on how much time is spent in prayer. Completing these readings each week will prepare the women for the discussion and activities of the group session.

About This Leader Guide

As you gather each week with the members of your group, you will have the opportunity to watch a video, discuss and respond to what you're learning, and pray together. You will need access to a television and DVD player with working remotes.

Creating a warm and inviting atmosphere will help make the women feel welcome. Although optional, you might consider providing snacks for your first meeting and inviting group members to rotate in bringing refreshments each week.

This leader guide and the DVD will be your primary tools for leading each group session. In this book you will find outlines for six group sessions, each formatted for either a 60-minute or 90-minute session:

60-Minute Format

Leader Prep	(Before the Session)
Welcome and Opening Prayer	5 minutes
Icebreaker	5 minutes
Video	15 minutes
Group Discussion	25 minutes
Closing Prayer	5–10 minutes

90-Minute Format

Leader Prep	(Before the Session)
Welcome and Opening Prayer	5–10 minutes
Icebreaker	5 minutes
Video	15 minutes
Group Discussion	35–40 minutes
Deeper Conversation	15 minutes
Closing Prayer	5–10 minutes

As you can see, the 90-minute format is identical to the 60-minute format but has more time for welcoming/fellowship and group discussion, plus a deeper conversation exercise for small groups. Feel free to adapt or modify either of these formats, as well as the individual segments and activities, in any way to meet the specific needs and preferences of your group.

Here is a brief overview of the elements included in both formats:

Leader Prep (Before the Session)

For your preparation prior to the group session, this section provides an overview of the week's Bible story and theme, the main point of the session, key Scriptures, and a list of materials and equipment needed. Be sure to review this section, as well as the session outline, before the group to plan and prepare. If you choose, you also may find it helpful to watch the DVD segment in advance.

Welcome and Opening Prayer (5–10 minutes, depending on session length)

To create a warm, welcoming environment as the women are gathering before the session begins, consider lighting one or more candles, providing coffee or other refreshments, and/or playing worship music. (Bring an iPod, smartphone, or tablet and a portable speaker if desired.) Be sure to provide name tags if the women do not know one another or you have new participants in your group. Then, when you are ready to begin, pray the opening prayer that is provided or offer your own.

Icebreaker (5 minutes)

Use the icebreaker to briefly engage the women in the topic while helping them feel comfortable with one another.

Video (about 15 minutes)

Next, watch the week's video segment together. Be sure to direct participants to the Video Viewer Guide in the participant workbook, which they may complete as they watch the video. (Answers are provided on page 61.)

Group Discussion (25–40 minutes, depending on session length)

After watching the video, choose from the questions provided to facilitate group discussion (questions are provided for both the video and the participant workbook). For the workbook portion, you may choose to read aloud the discussion points—which are excerpts from the participant workbook—or express them in your own words; then use one or more of the questions that follow to guide your conversation.

Note that more material is provided than you will have time to include. Before the session, select what you want to cover, putting a check mark beside it in your book. Reflect on each question and make some notes in the margins to share during your discussion time. Page references are provided for those questions that relate to specific questions or activities in the participant workbook. For these questions, invite group members to turn in their workbooks to the pages indicated. Participants will need Bibles in order to look up various supplementary Scriptures.

Depending on the number of women in your group and the level of their participation, you may not have time to cover everything you have selected, and that is okay. Rather than attempting to bulldoze through, follow the Spirit's lead and be open to where the Spirit takes the conversation. Remember that your role is not to have all the answers but to encourage discussion and sharing.

Deeper Conversation (15 minutes)

If your group is meeting for 90 minutes, move next to this exercise for deeper sharing in small groups, dividing into groups of two or three. This is a time for women to share more intimately and build connections with one another. (Encourage the women to break into different groups each week.) Before the session, write the question or questions you want to discuss on a markerboard or chart paper for all to see. Give a two-minute warning before time is up so that the groups may wrap up their discussion.

Closing Prayer (5–10 minutes)

Close by leading the group in prayer. Invite the women to briefly name prayer requests. To get things started, you might share a personal request of your own. As women share their requests, model for the group by writing each request in your participant workbook, indicating that you will remember to pray for them during the week.

As the study progresses, you might encourage members to participate in the Closing Prayer by praying out loud for one another and the requests given. Ask the women to volunteer to pray for specific requests, or have each woman pray for the woman on her right or left. Make sure name tags are visible so that group members do not feel awkward if they do not remember someone's name.

After the prayer, remind the women to pray for one another throughout the week.

Before You Begin

As we begin this journey together, you may be going into, living in the midst of, or coming out of a messy moment; or you may have a loved one who is. If so, hang on—you're not alone. The Bible is filled with examples for us to follow of people who not only endured messy lives but actually thrived with God's guidance, and you can too. So, get ready, because God is holding out His big, strong hands to you right in this moment and offering to take your messes and replace them with a masterpiece!

Jen

Basic Leader Helps

Preparing for the Sessions

- Check out your meeting space before each group session. Make sure the room is ready. Do you have enough chairs? Do you have the equipment and supplies you need? (See the list of materials needed in each session outline.)
- Pray for your group and each group member by name. Ask God to work in the life of every woman in your group.
- Read and complete the week's readings in the participant workbook and review the session outline in the leader guide. Put a check mark beside the discussion questions you want to cover and make any notes in the margins that you want to share in your discussion time. If you want, you may also choose to view the video segment.

Leading the Sessions

- Personally greet each woman as she arrives. If desired, take attendance. (This will assist you in identifying members who have missed several sessions so that you may contact them and let them know they were missed.)
- At the start of each session, ask the women to turn off or silence their cell phones.
- Always start on time. Honor the efforts of those who are on time.
- Encourage everyone to participate fully, but don't put anyone on the spot. Invite the women to share as they are comfortable. Be prepared to offer a personal example or answer if no one else responds at first.

- Facilitate but don't dominate. Remember that if you talk most of the time, group members may tend to listen passively rather than to engage personally.
- Try not to interrupt, judge, or minimize anyone's comments or input.
- Remember that you are not expected to be the expert or have all the answers. Acknowledge that all of you are on this journey together, with the Holy Spirit as your leader and guide. If issues or questions arise that you don't feel equipped to answer or handle, talk with the pastor or a staff member at your church.
- Encourage good discussion, but don't be timid about calling time on a particular question and moving ahead. Part of your responsibility is to keep the group on track. If you decide to spend extra time on a given question or activity, consider skipping or spending less time on another question or activity in order to stay on schedule.
- Try to end on time. If you are running over, give members the opportunity to leave if they need to. Then wrap up as quickly as you can.
- Be prepared for some women to want to hang out and talk at the end. If you need everyone to leave by a certain time, communicate this at the beginning of the session. If you are meeting in a church during regularly scheduled activities or have arranged for childcare, be sensitive to the agreed-upon ending time.
- Thank the women for coming, and let them know you're looking forward to seeing them next time.

Introductory Session

Note: This session is designed to be 60 minutes in length.

Leader Prep

Overview of the Session

This session is an opportunity to give an overview of the study; get to know one another and share hopes for the study; and handle some housekeeping details such as collecting information for a group roster (name, e-mail address, primary phone number, and, if desired, mailing address), making decisions regarding childcare and refreshments, and distributing books or providing instructions for purchasing. You also will watch a short video and pray together.

Note: Participants need to complete the devotional lessons for Week 1 prior to the session for Week 1.

Main Point of the Study

When we examine the lives of biblical heroes, we see that they were messy people just like us, who were used by God in powerful ways. As we dig into their stories, we will discover that we don't have to just endure messy lives but can actually thrive with God's guidance and help. In the hands of God, our messes can become masterpieces.

Key Scriptures

This means that anyone who belongs to Christ has become a new person. The old life is gone; a new life has begun! (2 Corinthians 5:17)

And I am certain that God, who began the good work within you, will continue his work until it is finally finished on the day when Christ Jesus returns. (Philippians 1:6)

What You Will Need
- *Messy People* DVD and a DVD player
- markerboard or chart paper and markers
- stick-on name tags and markers (optional)
- iPod, smartphone, or tablet and portable speaker (optional)

Session Outline

Welcome and Opening Prayer (10 minutes, depending on session length)

To create a warm, welcoming environment as the women are gathering before the session begins, consider lighting one or more candles, providing coffee or other refreshments, and/or playing worship music. (Bring an iPod, smartphone, or tablet and a portable speaker if desired.) Be sure to provide name tags if the women do not know one another or you have new participants in your group. Then, when you are ready to begin, pray the following prayer or offer your own:

Dear God, thank You for Your commitment and faithfulness to complete the work You have begun in us. Despite the messes of our lives, You make us new and transform us into the image of Your Son, Jesus. We invite You to do that work in us, Lord. We love You. Amen.

Icebreaker (5–10 minutes)

Invite the women to share short, "popcorn" responses to the following question:

- What is something messy that you enjoy, and what is something messy that you do *not* enjoy?

Video (5 minutes)

Play the Introductory Video segment on the DVD (duration: 3:39).

Group Discussion (25 minutes)

- Read aloud 2 Timothy 3:16-17. When we apply these verses to the lives of messy people in the Scriptures, what can we hope to gain from digging into their stories?
- Review the list of messy people we will be exploring in this study. Is there a particular kind of "mess" that you tend to associate with each one?
- Read aloud 2 Corinthians 5:17 and Philippians 1:6. What do these verses promise us, and how does this give you hope?

- What are your hopes for this study? What do you want to gain from it?

Closing Prayer (5–10 minutes)

Close the session by taking personal prayer requests from group members and leading the group in prayer. As you progress to later weeks in the study, you might encourage members to participate in the Closing Prayer by praying out loud for one another and the requests given.

Week 1

Rahab

Changing Your Messy Story
Joshua 2; 6

Leader Prep

Bible Story and Theme Overview

This week we explored the story of Rahab and the spies who needed her help. Rahab was a prostitute whom God used in a big way to change the course of Hebrew history. She was not Hebrew, but because of her faith in God, God rescued her—along with all of her family—and brought her into the family of God.

Main Point

The God of the universe chooses to use people with damaged reputations, broken hearts, and sinful pasts—and that is good news for us! He knows us, redeems us, and longs to bring us into His family, just as He did for Rahab.

Key Scriptures

Then Joshua secretly sent out two spies from the Israelite camp at Acacia Grove. He instructed them, "Scout out the land on the other side of the Jordan River, especially around Jericho." So the two men set out and came to the house of a prostitute named Rahab and stayed there that night.

(Joshua 2:1)

²But someone told the king of Jericho, "Some Israelites have come here tonight to spy out the land." ³So the king of Jericho sent orders to Rahab: "Bring out the men who have come into your house, for they have come here to spy out the whole land."

⁴Rahab had hidden the two men, but she replied, "Yes, the men were here earlier, but I didn't know where they were from. ⁵They left the town at dusk, as the gates were about to close. I don't know where they went. If you hurry, you can probably catch up with them." ⁶(Actually, she had taken them up to the roof and hidden them beneath bundles of flax she had laid out.) . . .

⁸Before the spies went to sleep that night, Rahab went up on the roof to talk with them. ⁹"I know the LORD has given you this land," she told them. "We are all afraid of you. Everyone in the land is living in terror. ¹⁰For we have heard how the LORD made a dry path for you through the Red Sea when you left Egypt. ¹¹. . . For the LORD your God is the supreme God of the heavens above and the earth below."

(Joshua 2:2-11)

What You Will Need
- *Messy People* DVD and a DVD player
- markerboard or chart paper and markers
- stick-on name tags and markers (optional)
- iPod, smartphone, or tablet and portable speaker (optional)

Session Outline

Welcome and Opening Prayer (5–10 minutes, depending on session length)
To create a warm, welcoming environment as the women are gathering before the session begins, consider lighting one or more candles, providing coffee or other refreshments, and/or playing worship music. (Bring an iPod, smartphone, or tablet and a portable speaker if desired.) Be sure to provide name tags if the women do not know one another or you have new participants in your group. Then, when you are ready to begin, pray the following prayer or offer your own:

Dear God, thank You for using messy people like us to accomplish Your work in this world. Help us to trust You with the kind of faith that Rahab had. May we experience Your presence with us as we study Your Word and share together. Amen.

Icebreaker (5 minutes)
Invite the women to share short, "popcorn" responses to the following question:

- What is your favorite fairytale princess? Why her?

Video (15 minutes)

Play the Week 1 video segment on the DVD. Invite participants to complete the Video Viewer Guide for Week 1 in the participant workbook as they watch (pages 36-37).

Group Discussion (25–40 minutes, depending on session length)

Note: More material is provided than you will have time to include. Before the session, select what you want to cover, putting a check mark beside it in your book. Page references are provided for questions related to questions or activities in the participant workbook. For these questions, invite participants to share the answers they wrote in their books.

Video Discussion Questions

- What was messy about Rahab's story? How did she change her story?
- Of the four simple, but not necessarily easy, steps that can help us move from mess to masterpiece, which resonates most with you right now, and why? (1. Recognize our need for God; 2. Resolve to lead a life that is centered in Christ; 3. Request help from godly people; 4. Remember Who holds your future.)
- How do you (or someone you love) need Jesus' help now to move from mess to best?

Participant Workbook Discussion Questions

1. No matter how messy your life has been, no matter what you've done or how your story has unfolded so far—God loves you, and you are chosen. Rahab's story is a great example of how God chooses to love and use messy people. (Day 1)

   - When have you felt chosen in life? How did it make you feel? (page 12)
   - What can we learn from Rahab's example about how God chooses and uses messy people?
   - In what ways, if any, does her story resonate with any experiences in your own life?

2. God chose to use Rahab in a very difficult situation; she was an unlikely accomplice to God's plan. This pagan woman, a prostitute

living in a Canaanite town, recognizes and has faith in the God of Israel. She believes in a God she does not personally know but respects because of His amazing miracles. She even goes so far as to declare "the LORD your God is the supreme God of the heavens above and the earth below" (Joshua 2:11). (Day 1)

- Read Ephesians 1:4 and John 15:16. What do these Scriptures teach you about God's view of you? (page 14)
- Read 1 Samuel 16:7. What does this verse tell us about how God sees us? (page 15)
- What does it mean for your life to know that God chooses you? (page 15)

3. The truth is that messy people come in all shapes and sizes. Our churches are full of them, because when we get right down to it, messy people are simply people with sin in their lives. (Day 2)

- Read Romans 3:23. Who are the messy people who sin? (page 18)
- Read Ephesians 2:10. According to this verse, why does God make us new creations in Jesus? (page 18)
- Do you have a dramatic testimony of coming to know Jesus, or did you grow up in the church? How have you seen God use all kinds of testimonies to draw people close to Him?

4. When presented with the opportunity to help God's people, Rahab is quick to respond in spite of her fears. In fact, she says her people are not only afraid but are living in *terror*. When you have the opportunity to serve God, there will be times when it is simple and sweet; but at other times, it will be terrifying. It will be messy, scary, and uncertain. That is when the opportunity for faith comes, and that is when heroines emerge. (Day 2)

- When God taps you on the heart, how quickly do you tend to respond? (page 20)
- When you consider how God might want to use you, what obstacles do you feel are holding you back? (page 20)
- How do you feel when you think of God using Rahab the prostitute? How do you feel when you think of God using *you*? (pages 20–21)

5. If I had been a resident of Jericho, would I have associated with Rahab? Would I have asked her about her life? Would we have been friends? Maybe, but probably not. Surely we would have hung out with different crowds. I mean, she would have been a messy person, right? But here's the problem. I'm messy too. I am just a different kind of messy. (Day 3)

    *   Read Mark 12:31. What did Jesus command us to do? Why do you think there is no greater commandment? (page 23)
    *   Have you ever had a time when you wanted someone to *really* see you—to notice the pain you're in and offer to intervene? If so, briefly describe that time. (page 23)
    *   What kinds of messy people make you uncomfortable? How do you respond to them? (page 23)

6. Jesus knows you. He knows your name—and what you weigh, no matter what your driver's license says! He knows about the dust bunnies under the stove and the bills you owe. And He cares. Jesus looks at *you* fresh each day and whispers, "I see you." (Day 3)

    *   As you consider that Jesus truly sees you and all that you are dealing with today, how does that make you feel? (page 25)
    *   Who has taken the time to really see you? (page 25)
    *   What can you do to see the unseen people around you every day? What are some small things you could do to acknowledge or communicate to them that you see them?

7. Being able to move forward in faith involves acknowledging our sin, repenting, and living in a way that honors God. (Day 4)

    *   Read 1 John 1:8. What does this in-your-face verse say we're doing if we claim to be without sin? (page 29)
    *   How does sin keep us from spiritual growth?
    *   Do you find it easy or difficult to acknowledge your sin to God? Why do you think that is?

8. At the end of Joshua 6, Rahab and her entire household are rescued. Because of her bold faithfulness, she and her family are redeemed. God has seen her faith, chosen her, used her, and redeemed her.

Now her story is changed forever. She overcomes the sins of her past and is used in new and powerful ways. (Day 4)

- Read 2 Corinthians 5:17. What does this verse tell us about what God can do with a messy past?
- How might God be wanting to change your story the way He changed Rahab's? (page 30)
- Who in your life may need your help to change their story? (page 30)

9. When Rahab first encounters the Israelite spies, she expresses faith in the power of their God. But when she moves into action for their God, He becomes her God. We don't know the details of what happens after Rahab is rescued in Jericho, but we do know that she becomes part of the Hebrew community. She marries and raises a family. She is changed. (Day 5)

- What did you learn about Rahab's family tree? See Matthew 1:5-6.
- Why is it significant that Rahab is included in the lineage of Jesus? What does that tell us about how God uses messy people?
- How does anyone caught in a difficult life situation move from messy to masterpiece?

10. Hebrews 11 is known as the Hall of Faith chapter. In this passage the writer lists some of the very greatest heroes of Scripture—all who had messy lives. And mentioned by name in this prestigious company is our heroine, Rahab! (Day 5)

- According to Hebrews 11:31, what saved Rahab? (page 34)
- Read James 2:25. How was Rahab viewed after she helped the spies? (page 34)
- Review the heroes of Hebrews 11 and some of the excuses they could have hidden behind. How does knowing the messiness of these heroes encourage you to trust God with your own messiness?

11. Think about all of your study and reflection this week.

- What thoughts or discoveries are sticking with you from this week's study?

Deeper Conversation (15 minutes)

Divide into smaller groups of two or three for deeper conversation. (Encourage the women to break into different groups each week.) Before the session, write on a markerboard or chart paper the question or questions you want the groups to discuss:

- What labels have you been given in life, and how have they affected you? (page 13)
- Have you ever felt disqualified from being used by God? (page 13) How has God used you anyway?

Give a two-minute warning before time is up so that the groups may wrap up their discussion.

Closing Prayer (5–10 minutes, depending on session length)

Close the session by taking personal prayer requests from group members and leading the group in prayer. As you progress to later weeks in the study, you might encourage members to participate in the Closing Prayer by praying out loud for one another and the requests given.

Week 2

The Prodigal Son

Restoring Messy Relationships
Luke 15:11-32

Leader Prep

Bible Story and Theme Overview

Through our study this week we have taken a look at the parable of the prodigal son in Luke 15 and considered five key steps in restoring messy relationships: coming to our senses, taking responsibility, running to reconcile, allowing for mistakes, and seeking peace. This parable shows us how to choose love, mercy, and peace in our messy relationships over bitterness, anger, and resentment.

Main Point

Rather than run away and rebel like the prodigal son or be judgmental and cold like the older brother, we can be the ones who run to restore what was broken. And as we do, it will bring a smile to God's face!

Key Scriptures

[11]"A man had two sons. [12]The younger son told his father, 'I want my share of your estate now before you die.' So his father agreed to divide his wealth between his sons.

[13]"A few days later this younger son packed all his belongings and moved to a distant land, and there he wasted all his money in wild living. [14]About the time his money ran out, a great famine swept over the land, and he began to starve. [15]He persuaded a local farmer to hire him, and the man sent him into his fields to feed the pigs. [16]The young man became so hungry that even the pods he was feeding the pigs looked good to him. But no one gave him anything.

[17]"When he finally came to his senses, he said to himself, 'At home even the hired servants have food enough to spare, and here I am dying of hunger! [18]I will go home to my father and say, "Father, I have sinned against both heaven and you, [19]and I am no longer worthy of being called your son. Please take me on as a hired servant." '

[20]"So he returned home to his father. And while he was still a long way off, his father saw him coming. Filled with love and compassion, he ran to his son, embraced him, and kissed him. [21]His son said to him, 'Father, I have sinned against both heaven and you, and I am no longer worthy of being called your son.'

[22]"But his father said to the servants, 'Quick! Bring the finest robe in the house and put it on him. Get a ring for his finger and sandals for his feet. [23]And kill the calf we have been fattening. We must celebrate with a feast, [24]for this son of mine was dead and has now returned to life. He was lost, but now he is found.' So the party began.

[25]"Meanwhile, the older son was in the fields working. When he returned home, he heard music and dancing in the house, [26]and he asked one of the servants what was going on. [27]'Your brother is back,' he was told, 'and your father has killed the fattened calf. We are celebrating because of his safe return.'

[28]"The older brother was angry and wouldn't go in. His father came out and begged him, [29]but he replied, 'All these years I've slaved for you and never once refused to do a single thing you told me to. And in all that time you never gave me even one young goat for a feast with my friends. [30]Yet when this son of yours comes back after squandering your money on prostitutes, you celebrate by killing the fattened calf!'

[31]"His father said to him, 'Look, dear son, you have always stayed by me, and everything I have is yours. [32]We had to celebrate this happy day. For your brother was dead and has come back to life! He was lost, but now he is found!' "

(Luke 15:11-32)

What You Will Need
- *Messy People* DVD and a DVD player
- markerboard or chart paper and markers

- stick-on name tags and markers (optional)
- iPod, smartphone, or tablet and portable speaker (optional)

Session Outline

Welcome and Opening Prayer (5–10 minutes, depending on session length)

To create a warm, welcoming environment as the women are gathering before the session begins, consider lighting one or more candles, providing coffee or other refreshments, and/or playing worship music. (Bring an iPod, smartphone, or tablet and a portable speaker if desired.) Be sure to provide name tags if the women do not know one another or you have new participants in your group. Then, when you are ready to begin, pray the following prayer or offer your own:

Dear God, thank You for loving us with a love that covers a multitude of sins. It is difficult for us to love when we've been hurt, but You continue to show us how. Give us insight and wisdom as we study Your Word and learn to love deeply as You love us. Amen.

Icebreaker (5 minutes)

Invite the women to share short, "popcorn" responses to the following question:

- What is the most precious thing you've ever lost? Describe your search and feelings after either finding it or giving up the search.

Video (15 minutes)

Play the Week 2 video segment on the DVD. Invite participants to complete the Video Viewer Guide for Week 2 in the participant workbook as they watch (pages 65–66).

Group Discussion (25–40 minutes, depending on session length)

Note: More material is provided than you will have time to include. Before the session, select what you want to cover, putting a check mark beside it in your book. Page references are provided for questions related to questions or activities in the participant workbook. For these questions, invite participants to share the answers they wrote in their books.

Video Discussion Questions

- How much energy do you waste on worry?
- Imagine how the father of the prodigal son must have felt when his son asked for his inheritance. How would you feel about that? How would you respond?

- Of the five simple, but not necessarily easy, tips for restoring messy relationships, which resonates most with you right now, and why? (1. Make the first move; 2. Own your stuff; 3. Listen carefully; 4. Speak kindly; 5. Focus on reconciliation and not just resolution.)

Participant Workbook Discussion Questions

1. What keeps me up at night is worrying about broken relationships. With God's help through prayer, I can deal with people who are having a crisis, battling cancer, or grieving the loss of a loved one— and even deal with my own grief and sadness. But if I am involved in a messy relationship, it literally wakes me up at night. (Day 1)

    - What broken relationships have kept you up at night? (page 41)
    - What kinds of things make a relationship messy?
    - Read Luke 15:11-32. What kind of messy relationships do we see here?

2. No one is exempt from sin. Recognizing our own sin is the first step in repairing broken relationships. So when the prodigal son comes to his senses, recognizing his own sin, it is the beginning of restoration. (Day 1)

    - Read Romans 3:23. Who is exempt from sin? (page 42)
    - Why is recognizing our own sin a first step toward restoration?
    - Read 1 Peter 4:8. How have you known this to be true in your own relationships?
    - What are some first steps toward peacemaking when a relationship has been broken?

3. Galatians 6:5 teaches us that "we are each responsible for our own conduct." In order to build strong, healthy relationships, we must be willing to step up and be responsible for those times when we blow it. But in order to do that, we have to overcome a nasty obstacle: pride. (Day 2)

    - How does pride sometimes show up in your relationships? How does it mess up relationships?
    - As you consider the story of the prodigal son, where do you see pride rearing its head?

4. When the prodigal son decides to admit his sin and return home, he humbles himself. Humility is the opposite of pride. It is noble—putting your rights aside for the greater good of others. Humility will lead you to say powerful things: "I am sorry. I was wrong. Please forgive me. How can I make things better?" (Day 2)

   - Read Colossians 3:12-13 and Matthew 6:14-15. According to these verses, why is it important to humble ourselves and seek forgiveness? (page 47)
   - Do you find it easy or difficult to ask forgiveness when you have caused a break in a relationship?
   - Which do you think is more difficult: asking forgiveness or granting forgiveness? Why?

5. Run to people. Love them with abandon. It doesn't matter who is watching. Run, because love matters. We see this truth in the parable of the prodigal son. (Day 3)

   - Would you say you tend to be guarded with people who have hurt you, or do you love with abandon?
   - What do we learn from the father of the prodigal son about the role of mercy in messy relationships?
   - How can we grow in our capacity to love and forgive?

6. No matter what you've done or who you've hurt, God loves you. He loves you enough to send His Son so that He can have a relationship with you. He is not angry with you. He watches from a long way off, hoping to see you coming toward Him. And when He does, He runs to meet you! (Day 3)

   - Read John 3:16-17 and Romans 5:8. What do these verses have to teach us about God's passionate pursuit of prodigal people? (page 52)
   - What has been your predominant image of God over the course of your Christian walk? Do you see God as angry or as passionate in His affection and mercy for you?
   - What does the father's example of running to his son teach us about extending forgiveness?

7. Bitterness and anger will eat you up. Discouragement and depression will leave you sad. Waiting for someone else to make things right is a waste of energy. The only person you really have control over is yourself. So determine in advance how you will respond when relationships get messy. (Day 4)

   • When someone hurts you, intentionally or not, how do you usually respond? What's your go-to emotion? (page 56)
   • How do bitterness and anger eat a person up?
   • Read Ephesians 4:31-32. What are we to avoid? What are some attitudes and actions we are to have toward others? (page 56)

8. Forgiveness is not overlooking or condoning sin. It is not pretending that the hurt isn't real. That would be wrong. It is simply saying, "What happened is wrong, but I choose not to be angry and bitter about it. I choose to love you while still holding you accountable for your behavior." (Day 4)

   • How have you experienced the truth of Colossians 3:13 and 1 Peter 4:8—on both the giving and the receiving ends? How have forgiveness and deep love affected your own life? (page 58)
   • Look back at Luke 15:28-30. Try to put yourself in the older brother's shoes and be honest: how do you think you would have reacted? (page 58)
   • What does it look like to love someone deeply while still holding them accountable for their sin against you? Is the first step justice or mercy? Why?

9. Part of being human is dealing with relationships when they get messy. When there is hurt, betrayal, and disappointment, we get to choose how we will respond. Learning good communication skills and going out of our way to develop healthy patterns in dealing with others is a burden that the Christ-follower must bear in order to serve Jesus well. (Day 5)

- Read John 13:34-35. How would you describe what it means to love as Jesus loved? Practically speaking, what does this look like? (page 62)
- In arguments with people you love, do you try to win? How is mutual winning achieved so that there is no loser?
- Why does the way we show love help the world to know we are Jesus' disciples? Would you say your current messy relationships are examples of loving as Jesus loved? Why or why not?

10. The parable of the prodigal son is actually a story of two lost boys. First there is the prodigal, the younger son who wastes his inheritance on living a wild life. And then there is the older brother, who is angry that there is celebration for his sinful sibling. In both situations we see a father who seeks what is lost. The loving father is proactive in reaching out to his lost sons. We don't see him hesitate to love both of his boys deeply. (Day 5)

- How is the father in this parable like our heavenly Father?
- What does it mean to you that the father showed grace and love for *both* sons?
- What is the father's first response to both boys? How can we mature in our faith so that love is always our first response?

11. Think about all of your study and reflection this week.

- What thoughts or discoveries are sticking with you from this week's study?

Deeper Conversation (15 minutes)

Divide into smaller groups of two or three for deeper conversation. (Encourage the women to break into different groups each week.) Before the session, write on a markerboard or chart paper the question or questions you want the groups to discuss:

- A loving father, a prodigal son, and a resentful brother: which do you most relate to today? Why? (page 64)
- Read Hebrews 12:14. What does it look like for us to "work at living in peace"? What are some ways that you can begin right now to work at living in peace?

Give a two-minute warning before time is up so that the groups may wrap up their discussion.

Closing Prayer (5–10 minutes)

Close the session by taking personal prayer requests from group members and leading the group in prayer. As you progress to later weeks in the study, you might encourage members to participate in the Closing Prayer by praying out loud for one another and the requests given.

Week 3

Josiah

Breaking Messy Family Cycles
2 Kings 22–23; 2 Chronicles 34–35

Leader Prep

Bible Story and Theme Overview

This week we looked at the story of Josiah in 2 Kings 22–23 and 2 Chronicles 34–35 and explored how he was able to break away from his messy past in order to create a new future for his people. We also explored how to grow closer to Christ by examining our lives, identifying destructive patterns, and beginning to get rid of excuses, habits, and sins that keep us from God's best for our lives. One way to increase our chances of living a Christlike life is to build a team. Our odds of success are significantly strengthened when we join with other Christ-followers toward a common goal.

Main Point

When we take time to sort through life's messes, examine our lives, and put things in order, the future holds the promise of new blessings.

Key Scriptures

[1]*Josiah was eight years old when he became king, and he reigned in Jerusalem thirty-one years.* [2]*He did what was right in the eyes of the LORD and followed the ways of his father David, not turning aside to the right or to the left.*

[3]*In the eighth year of his reign, while he was still young, he began to seek the God of his father David. In his twelfth year he began to purge Judah and Jerusalem of high places, Asherah poles and idols....*

[8]*In the eighteenth year of Josiah's reign, to purify the land and the temple, he sent Shaphan son of Azaliah and Maaseiah the ruler of the city, with Joah son of Joahaz, the recorder, to repair the temple of the LORD his God.*

(2 Chronicles 34:1-3, 8 NIV)

Instead, let us test and examine our ways.
Let us turn back to the LORD.
(Lamentations 3:40)

[23]*Search me, O God, and know my heart;*
test me and know my anxious thoughts.
[24]*Point out anything in me that offends you,*
and lead me along the path of everlasting life.
(Psalm 139:23-24)

What You Will Need

- *Messy People* DVD and a DVD player
- markerboard or chart paper and markers
- stick-on name tags and markers (optional)
- iPod, smartphone, or tablet and portable speaker (optional)

Session Outline

Welcome and Opening Prayer (5 minutes)

To create a warm, welcoming environment as the women are gathering before the session begins, consider lighting one or more candles, providing coffee or other refreshments, and/or playing worship music. (Bring an iPod, smartphone, or tablet and a portable speaker if desired.) Be sure to provide name tags if the women do not know one another or you have new participants in your group. Then, when you are ready to begin, pray the following prayer or offer your own:

Dear God, thank You for new beginnings. Thank You that You continue to call us out of our mess and into the future You have in store for each of us. Help us not to make excuses but to follow where You lead. Speak to us now as we seek to understand Your Word. Amen.

Icebreaker (5 minutes)

Invite the women to share short, "popcorn" responses to the following question:

- What is your best habit and your worst habit?

Video (15 minutes)

Play the Week 3 video segment on the DVD. Invite participants to complete the Video Viewer Guide for Week 3 in the participant workbook as they watch (pages 99–100).

Group Discussion (25–40 minutes, depending on session length)

Note: More material is provided than you will have time to include. Before the session, select what you want to cover, putting a check mark beside it in your book. Page references are provided for questions related to questions or activities in the participant workbook. For these questions, invite participants to share the answers they wrote in their books.

Video Discussion Questions

- How do old patterns keep us from God's best for our lives?
- Which of the four steps to break the cycle of old bad habits is the most difficult for you, and why? (1. Don't procrastinate; 2. Don't play the victim; 3. Remove temptation; 4. Give God control.)
- In what way is it your choice whether or not you break unhealthy cycles and live your best life? What role does God play in the process?

Participant Workbook Discussion Questions

1. Life is full of messes. But when we take time to sort through life's messes and put things in order, the future holds the promise of new blessings. (Day 1)

    - Read Lamentations 3:40. What do you think it means to "test and examine our ways"? How might this help us to turn back to the Lord? (page 70)
    - Do you prefer to hide the mess or get everything all out in the open? Which do you think is better and why?
    - What kind of family messes have you seen passed on from generation to generation?

2. The examples that had been set for Josiah were poor ones. His father and grandfather had not honored the Lord. But Josiah looked beyond what he knew as normal to examine the values and practices within his culture. Then as God's Word was revealed to him, he made the decisions necessary to put things back into right order. (Day 1)

- In your own words, piece together the details of Josiah's story that you read in 2 Chronicles 34–35. What are some significant moments?
- Read 2 Chronicles 34:19. What did Josiah do when he heard the words of the Law? (page 72) Why was he so grieved?
- In what ways is it difficult to separate from a past mess and begin a new future? What is required to take those steps?

3. It would have been easy for Josiah to come up with excuses for why he was not up to the job of kingdom reformation. But instead he sought the one true God, removed the pagan idols, and rebuilt the temple for worship. He personally recommitted himself to God and then led his entire nation to do the same. For Josiah, there were no excuses. (Day 2)

- Do you find yourself making excuses for why you can't do the work God has called you to do? Why do you think we make so many excuses for so many things?
- Read Ephesians 6:10. What makes us strong? How does this verse apply to our messes and bad habits? (page 77)
- Read the two translations of 1 Timothy 4:7b on page 78 in the workbook. How might this verse direct your daily life? (page 78)

4. When we learn a new skill or develop a new habit, there is a learning curve. It's during that time that we have to be the most disciplined and determined. As we examine our lives and seek the steps we need to take to move toward holiness, we must get rid of anything that would hold us back. No excuses. (Day 2)

- Read Hebrews 12:1. What word is used to describe what slows us down, including sin? (page 79)
- How is sin (our bad habits) like a weight that slows us down?
- Read Proverbs 8:5. How can we "learn" to be mature, to let go of excuses and move toward holiness?

5. Every day you decide who will be in control of your life. Will it be you or God? God has the bigger picture of your life in mind. He sees things that you cannot see and wants to guide you in ways that you cannot yet understand. His plans are better than yours, just as they are better than mine. The question is, will you trust that He is looking out for you even when you can't understand all that is happening in your life? (Day 3)

   - Do you find it easy or difficult to surrender to whatever plans God has for you? Why?
   - Read Psalm 46:10. What are we to let go of, and what will be the result when we do? (page 83)
   - Read Isaiah 55:8-9. How does this verse give you wisdom or comfort for those times when you can't understand what is happening in your life? (page 83)

6. There is a time to plan—a time to strategize, pray, and learn. But there also is a time to move. As you pursue dreams, take the time to learn, gather wise counsel, develop a plan, and establish time lines; but don't be too afraid to get started. Far too many dreams die in the waiting stage. Don't allow the desire for perfection to become fuel for procrastination. We live in a less-than-perfect world, so we are forced to follow God in less-than-perfect circumstances. Do it anyway! (Day 3)

   - Why do you think many dreams die in the waiting stage? Do you have an example from personal experience?
   - If you knew you wouldn't fail, what would you attempt for God's glory in your life? (page 85)
   - Read Ecclesiastes 11:4. How have you known this to be true in your life?

7. Josiah chose to break the pattern. He did not want to repeat the same sins of his ancestors. He not only had the courage to confront sin and break the patterns of sin in his family and country; he also encouraged them to return wholeheartedly to obeying God's instructions. What a great life lesson for us today. God's Word is meant to be a road map, a guide toward wisdom and living into God's favor. (Day 4)

- Read Psalm 119:9. What does this verse tell us about living in a way that pleases the Lord?
- Read Job 32:7. Should we read this as a promise of wisdom or as the possibility of increasing wisdom? Is it possible to grow older but not wiser? If so, how does that happen?
- What wisdom have you gained as a result of poor choices in your past?

8. Most people have a "pet sin." A pet sin is one that hangs around and attaches itself to you. Instead of shooing it away, like a wild raccoon at your back door, you welcome it with a bowl of milk; and pretty soon that critter becomes rabid and takes up residence in your life. It bites you regularly, but it has become part of your life; and to make it leave would take work. So you make excuses for its behavior and try to keep it hidden because you know others wouldn't think it's a good idea to keep it around. (Day 4)

- Without getting too personal, how did it feel to examine your heart for your pet sin this week?
- Read Romans 7:15, 17-18. Is this an excuse? Explain your response. (pages 88-89) Do you relate to Paul's struggle? Why or why not?
- Read Romans 7:24-25; Romans 8:2; and Galatians 5:16. What insights do these verses give us regarding the answer to the problem of sin? (page 89)

9. One way to increase our chances of living a Christlike life is to build a team. Our odds of success are significantly strengthened when we join with other Christ-followers toward a common goal. (Day 5)

- Do you prefer to work alone or on a team? Why?
- Read Ecclesiastes 4:9-10. According to these verses, what are the benefits of working together? (page 91)
- Recall a time of need in your life when others came to help. How did it affect your relationships? (page 91)

10. Together, working as a team, we are stronger. In ministry, parenting, friendships, careers, and even small groups, we accomplish more and go further when we work side by side. There is strength in doing life together. (Day 5)

- Read Romans 12:15 and Ecclesiastes 4:12. According to these verses, what are some of the reasons for doing life together? What are some of the benefits? (page 96)
- Read Proverbs 18:24; 27:6. What do these verses tell us about a true friend? (page 97)
- What are some times in your life when you felt stronger because you had the strength of others helping you along?

11. Think about all of your study and reflection this week.

- What thoughts or discoveries are sticking with you from this week's study?

Deeper Conversation (15 minutes)

Divide into smaller groups of two or three for deeper conversation. (Encourage the women to break into different groups each week.) Before the session, write on a markerboard or chart paper the question or questions you want the groups to discuss:

- What spiritual gifts and other unique skills and abilities has God gifted *you* with? If you are not sure, ask family members or friends what gifts they have observed in you. (page 95)
- What are some ways you can use those gifts for God's kingdom? How have you used them in the past in your church or community? (page 95)
- When is a time you served outside of your comfort zone? How did it go? (page 96)

Give a two-minute warning before time is up so that the groups may wrap up their discussion.

Closing Prayer (5–10 minutes)

Close the session by taking personal prayer requests from group members and leading the group in prayer. As you progress to later weeks in the study, you might encourage members to participate in the Closing Prayer by praying out loud for one another and the requests given.

Week 4

Mary

Surviving Life's Messy Plot Twists
Luke 1:26-38

Leader Prep

Bible Story and Theme Overview

This week we've looked at Mary, the mother of Jesus, and the qualities in her life that made her usable in messy situations, asking ourselves this question: "Why did God choose Mary to be favored among women?" We discovered that she was available, interruptible, trustworthy, and courageous. And we explored how we, too, can be used by God in mighty ways—even when our lives get messy and do not go as planned.

Main Point

God is looking for people who are available, interruptible, trustworthy, and courageous. When we turn our hearts fully toward Him as laborers in God's fields, miraculous results are produced!

Key Scriptures

[26]God sent the angel Gabriel to Nazareth, a village in Galilee, [27]to a virgin named Mary. She was engaged to be married to a man named Joseph, a descendant of King David. [28]Gabriel appeared to her and said, "Greetings, favored woman! The Lord is with you!"

[29]Confused and disturbed, Mary tried to think what the angel could mean. [30]"Don't be afraid, Mary," the angel told her, "for you have found favor with God! [31]You will conceive and give birth to a son, and you will name him Jesus. [32]He will be very great and will be called the Son of the Most High. . . ."

[34]Mary asked the angel, "But how can this happen? I am a virgin."

[35]The angel replied, "The Holy Spirit will come upon you. . . . The baby to be born will be holy, and he will be called the Son of God. . . . [37]For the word of God will never fail."

[38]Mary responded, "I am the Lord's servant. May everything you have said about me come true."

(Luke 1:26-38)

What You Will Need

- *Messy People* DVD and a DVD player
- markerboard or chart paper and markers
- stick-on name tags and markers (optional)
- iPod, smartphone, or tablet and portable speaker (optional)

Session Outline

Welcome and Opening Prayer (5–10 minutes, depending on session length)

To create a warm, welcoming environment as the women are gathering before the session begins, consider lighting one or more candles, providing coffee or other refreshments, and/or playing worship music. (Bring an iPod, smartphone, or tablet and a portable speaker if desired.) Be sure to provide name tags if the women do not know one another or you have new participants in your group. Then, when you are ready to begin, pray the following prayer or offer your own:

Dear God, thank You for interruptions and plot twists that send us on Your path. Give us courage to say yes when You call to us. As we gather to listen to Your Word and to one another, open our spiritual eyes and ears to what You would have us learn. Amen.

Icebreaker (5 minutes)

Invite the women to share short, "popcorn" responses to the following question:

- What is a favorite story of yours (whether a book or movie) that took an unexpected turn?

Video (15 minutes)

Play the Week 4 video segment on the DVD. Invite participants to complete the Video Viewer Guide for Week 4 in the participant workbook as they watch (page 130).

Group Discussion (25–40 minutes, depending on session length)

Note: More material is provided than you will have time to include. Before the session, select what you want to cover, putting a check mark beside it in your book. Page references are provided for questions related to questions or activities in the participant workbook. For these questions, invite participants to share the answers they wrote in their books.

Video Discussion Questions

- What does Mary teach us about being available to God?
- What are some practical ways we can honor God and live by His standards rather than conform to the expectations of the world around us? Why is this necessary if we want to be used by God to make a difference in the world around us?
- What do you see in the world that needs to change? What has God been wanting to partner with you to do?
- When we don't understand God's instructions or timing, what are the next right steps?
- What does it mean to stay "usable" to God?

Participant Workbook Discussion Questions

1. We will experience difficulties in life. Sometimes they are just inconveniences such as having a dead car battery or working late. But other times these difficulties that creep into our lives can disrupt our plans entirely. Cancer, job loss, a betrayal, or an accident are just some examples of life interruptions that can step in and shake our world. (Day 1)

   - When has your life taken an unexpected turn (whether good or bad), and how did you respond initially? When has life dealt you a *crushing* disappointment? (pages 104–105)

- Read John 16:33. What does Jesus say that we can expect to experience, and what is the good news He gives us? (page 105)
- How does the promise of John 16:33 give you peace when bad things happen in your life or the world?

2. Mary's story looks beautiful in stained glass windows. She looks serene in Christmas nativity sets. But in reality her life had many difficulties and often must have seemed very messy. Surely she was ostracized in Nazareth as an unwed teen. Mary's life was messy, just as our lives are. Yet through it all she was faithful. (Day 1)

- Read Luke 1:28-32. Why do you think the angel called Mary a "favored woman"? What might that mean? (page 106)
- Read Matthew 2:13-14. What must it have been like for Mary to flee to another country to protect her child from King Herod?
- What are some other examples of the messiness of Mary's story?

3. Mary said yes to God, and saying yes to God means being available. (Day 2)

- Read Luke 1:38. How does Mary's response reveal her availability? (page 110)
- Recall a time when God wanted to use you. Were there any questions you wanted to have answered before you said yes? If so, what were they? (page 110)
- What questions would you have had for God if you were in Mary's shoes?

4. Just as God is always available to us as our Father, Friend, and Savior, we have the opportunity to be available to Him. Mary was available, and as a result she played an integral role in the redemption story of the human race. God has a role for you to play also. (Day 2)

- How available are *you* when it comes to hearing and responding to God's voice? (page 111)
- Would you be willing to tell God in advance that you are available to be used by Him? Explain your response. (page 111)
- What does Jesus teach us about being available to God?

5.   In the prayer that He taught His disciples, Jesus models for us how we should pray and, to some degree, how we should set goals. He doesn't say "My will be done" but "Thy will be done" (Matthew 6:10 KJV). Replacing our will with God's will and remaining interruptible is part of the secret to being used in miraculous ways in this life! (Day 3)

-   What plans have you made for yourself that God has replaced with better ones? (page 114)
-   How has praying for God's will to be done blessed you? Recall a specific situation if you can. (page 114)
-   Has pursuing your will versus God's will ever caused you to stumble? If so, explain briefly. (page 115)

6.   Throughout Jesus' ministry, He was constantly interrupted. When people sought Jesus, He was not only available, He was interruptible. He didn't scold people for wanting to get close to Him. He was patient with the children. He didn't complain when the roof was torn apart. And He didn't fuss when the woman touched the hem of His robe for healing. He was available and interruptible. (Day 3)

-   When your plans are interrupted, how do you usually feel? How interruptible is your schedule right now? (page 115)
-   How might your life be enriched if you determined to always be interruptible? (page 116)
-   When have interruptions turned to plot twists in the story of your life?

7.   Long before Mary was pregnant with Jesus, she said, "Yes, God, I am available and interruptible; and I can be trusted with Your will for my life." Saying yes to God means being trustworthy. (Day 4)

-   When has God trusted you with a task that seemed much too large for you? (page 120)
-   What gifts (people, resources, and abilities) has God entrusted to you? (page 121)
-   What does it mean to you to know that God trusts you with these things?

8. Mary wasn't only there for the birthday parties and the awards days at school—or whatever the ordinary, everyday experiences of Jesus' life were. She was there when others fled. She was there in the good times as well as in the bad times that surely must have crushed her heart. Why? Because, like most mothers, she loved her son. But I believe it also was because she loved God. She had been entrusted with the responsibility of Jesus' care, and she was not going to let God down. Mary was trustworthy with the task that God had put before her. (Day 4)

    *   Read John 19:25, and let these words sink in. What must that experience have been like for Mary? What must she have been feeling? How would you have felt in her place? (page 122)
    *   What task or responsibility has God put before you? (page 122)
    *   Read 2 Chronicles 16:9. According to this verse, what kind of people is God looking for, and what does He promise to do for them? (page 123)

9. If you are to be available, interruptible, and trustworthy so that you can say yes to God, then you are going to need courage—because moving from your will into God's will can be a scary, overwhelming endeavor. It will move you outside your comfort zone, requiring you to move in faith against the fears that are holding you back. (Day 5)

    *   What fears have kept you from being used by God in the past? (page 126)
    *   What fears do you continue to confront? (page 126)
    *   Read Luke 1:26-30. What was Mary's reaction to the angel's news in verse 29? What words would you use to describe her at this point in the story? (page 126) What fears must have rushed through her heart?

10. Even when we are available, interruptible, trustworthy, and courageous—even when we are following God's plan—life can still be messy. Faithful people encounter messy situations. Mary certainly did. Her role in God's plan brought both joy and sadness and must have seemed messy at times. Yet it was because she was available, interruptible, trustworthy, and courageous that she was able to

partner with God in the greatest rescue mission of all time! God wants to partner with you too. (Day 5)

- If you knew that you had nothing to be afraid of, what would you attempt today for God? (page 129)
- Discuss your answers to the chart on page 128. Are you happy with your availability to God or did you discover an area of needed growth?
- Would you say you trust God completely for whatever mission God has for you? Why or why not?

11. Think about all of your study and reflection this week.

- What thoughts or discoveries are sticking with you from this week's study?

Deeper Conversation (15 minutes)

Divide into smaller groups of two or three for deeper conversation. (Encourage the women to break into different groups each week.) Before the session, write on a markerboard or chart paper the question or questions you want the groups to discuss:

- At the end of Week 3, we looked briefly at spiritual gifts. Review the gifts you listed and the ways you've used them in your church or community. (page 95) What are some specific ways you have used all of the gifts at your disposal—spiritual gifts, abilities, talents, and resources—to help others? Describe a few examples. (page 123)
- How have fear or interruptions kept you from using your gifts for God?

Give a two-minute warning before time is up so that the groups may wrap up their discussion.

Closing Prayer (5–10 minutes)

Close the session by taking personal prayer requests from group members and leading the group in prayer. Encourage members to participate in the Closing Prayer by praying out loud for one another and the requests given.

Week 5

Overcoming the Mess of Criticism
1 Samuel 16–18; 2 Samuel 12; 15

Leader Prep

Bible Story and Theme Overview

This week we've explored the messy story of King David, who had to learn when to ignore criticism (such as when his own brothers mocked his bravery in confronting Goliath) and when to listen (such as when the prophet Nathan confronted him with his sins of adultery and murder).

Main Point

When God gives us an important assignment, there are sure to be naysayers telling us that we're the wrong person, we've got the wrong idea, we're doing it the wrong way, or we're just not good enough. But like David, if we keep our eyes on God we can overcome criticism with confidence.

Key Scriptures

⁵I depend on God alone;
  I put my hope in him.
⁶He alone protects and saves me;
  he is my defender,
  and I shall never be defeated.
⁷My salvation and honor depend on God;
  he is my strong protector;
  he is my shelter.
                    (Psalm 62:5-7 GNT)

Wounds from a friend can be trusted,
  but an enemy multiplies kisses.
              (Proverbs 27:6 NIV)

⁵David was furious. "As surely as the LORD lives," he vowed, "any man who would do such a thing deserves to die! ⁶He must repay four lambs to the poor man for the one he stole and for having no pity."

⁷Then Nathan said to David, "You are that man!"

                                        (2 Samuel 12:5-7)

What You Will Need

- *Messy People* DVD and a DVD player
- markerboard or chart paper and markers
- stick-on name tags and markers (optional)
- iPod, smartphone, or tablet and portable speaker (optional)

Session Outline

Welcome and Opening Prayer (5–10 minutes, depending on session length)

To create a warm, welcoming environment as the women are gathering before the session begins, consider lighting one or more candles, providing coffee or other refreshments, and/or playing worship music. (Bring an iPod, smartphone, or tablet and a portable speaker if desired.) Be sure to provide name tags if the women do not know one another or you have new participants in your group. Then, when you are ready to begin, pray the following prayer or offer your own:

Dear God, thank You for good friends who tell us the truth about where and how we need to grow in our walk with You. Make us aware of Your presence now and teach us to listen for Your voice above all the messiness of life. Amen.

Icebreaker (5 minutes)

Invite the women to share short, "popcorn" responses to the following question:

- What is your immediate, gut-level response when you are criticized for something? Rage? Tears? Remorse? Revenge?

Video (15 minutes)

Play the Week 5 video segment on the DVD. Invite participants to complete the Video Viewer Guide for Week 5 in the participant workbook as they watch (pages 166–167).

Group Discussion (25–40 minutes, depending on session length)

Note: More material is provided than you will have time to include. Before the session, select what you want to cover, putting a check mark beside it in your book. Page references are provided for questions related to questions or activities in the participant workbook. For these questions, invite participants to share the answers they wrote in their books.

Video Discussion Questions

- Of the five ways that we can respond to criticism in a Christlike way, which comes most naturally to you? Which is most difficult for you, and why? (1. Listen carefully; 2. Stay cool; 3. Process the information; 4. Learn what you can; 5. Pray about it.)
- What is the difference between helpful truth-telling and having a critical spirit?
- What does it look like to offer criticism with love? Why is this important?

Participant Workbook Discussion Questions

1. You simply cannot please everyone. There are always going to be people in your life who criticize you and speak against you. It's inevitable. You will be misunderstood, misquoted, unfairly judged, attacked, and gossiped about. It's part of life on planet earth. If you are swayed by every opinion, you will not live a very fruitful life. You cannot allow every criticism to determine how you will live. (Day 1)

   - When was the last time you were criticized, attacked, or judged? Briefly describe the situation and how it made you feel. (page 135)
   - How do you typically respond when criticized? (page 136)

- Ideally, what would you like your response to be when criticized? (page 136)

2. As a teenager David had to learn to deal with critics, which he did by trusting and relying on God. From then on, critics would be his constant companion throughout his life. Through it all, David always turned to God for strength and truth. (Day 1)

   - Read Psalm 62:5-7. How does David describe God in these verses? (page 138)
   - What are some examples from Scripture of David dealing with critics?
   - When have you known God to be your defender, protector, or shield?

3. Jesus is our example of how to respond to hurts. Throughout His ministry, He was surrounded by critics and those who plotted to destroy him. (Day 2)

   - Read 1 Peter 2:23. What did Jesus do when He was hurt by others? (page 141)
   - Read Luke 23:34. What was Jesus' response on the cross to those who were crucifying Him? (page 142)
   - What are some challenges we face when trying to follow Jesus' example? Share from personal experience if you are willing.

4. It's important to recognize that we too have a choice to make when we face difficulties in life. Usually we are unable to control the situations around us, although that's often what we want to do. But what we can do is control our response to those situations. (Day 2)

   - Read 1 Samuel 24:1-7 and 1 Samuel 26:7-12. What does David decide to do on each occasion, and what reason does he give? Do you find it hard not to defend yourself when attacked? Why or why not? (pages 143–144)
   - What are some practical things you can do in the moment to keep from fighting back or speaking unkindly? (page 145)
   - Are there times when God might want us to remain silent when under attack? Explain your response. (page 145)

5. We need people in our lives who can speak deep truths to us—even when those truths are constructive criticism. (Day 3)

   - When and how have wounds from a friend been helpful in your life? (page 148)
   - Read Proverbs 27:6. Why do we need friends who tell us the truth, even if it hurts?
   - What does it take to build a friendship so strong that it can withstand difficult truth-telling?

6. David and Nathan provide a good example for us of the right way to give and receive constructive criticism. Nathan obediently delivered a difficult message to someone in authority. It was God's message, not his own; and he stuck with the script given to him by the Lord without offering his own opinions and commentary. David did not make excuses or become angry when his sins were revealed. He was repentant and accepted both the consequences for his disobedience and the forgiveness of the God he loved. (Day 3)

   - Do you generally wait for the Lord to tell you if, when, and how to give critical feedback, or do you tend to forge ahead on your own? Why is it important to wait on the Lord? (page 150)
   - How would you describe the tone you tend to use when you offer criticism? (page 150)
   - Read Proverbs 13:17 and Proverbs 27:17. What do these Scriptures teach us about the types of people we should choose for close friendships? (page 152)

7. David had to learn when to ignore criticism, such as when his own brothers mocked his bravery in confronting Goliath, and when to listen, such as he did when the prophet Nathan confronted him with his sins of adultery and murder. And we must learn to do the same. The key is in evaluating the source or motivation of the critic. (Day 4)

   - What distracts you from focusing on God? (page 154)
   - Read Matthew 14:22-32. What is Peter's "calling" in this story? (page 154) What happened when Peter got distracted?
   - How do we learn when to ignore criticism and when to listen?

8. All criticism is not created equally. Some is meant to sharpen us; some is meant to hurt us. Some comes from jealousy and attempts to distract us from completing what God has called us to do; some comes from a deeply rooted love. There is wisdom in evaluating the criticism we receive in order to determine the motivation so that we can know what to keep and what to discard. (Day 4)

   • What are some examples of criticism that would sharpen us? What are some examples of criticism that is meant to harm?
   • Recall a time recently when you were criticized or critiqued. Do you believe it was meant to help or to hurt, and why? What do you think was the person's motivation? (page 157) (Be sure to use discretion when sharing about others.)
   • List some examples from Scripture of people who were out to harm David.

9. In 2 Samuel 6 we read the account of David dancing and praising the Lord as the ark of the covenant is brought into Jerusalem. As his wife Michal looks down from her window and sees David rejoicing, she is not pleased with what she views as un-kingly behavior. She is critical, even showing disgust and contempt for David. But he is not swayed. (Day 5)

   • Read 2 Samuel 6:22. What was David's response to Michal's criticism? What do you think he meant by this? (page 161)
   • Have you ever looked like a fool for God? If so, when and how? (page 162)
   • Read Proverbs 15:2. According to this verse, who was the real fool— Michal or David? Explain your answer. (page 162)

10. Every great opportunity comes with opposition. When we attempt anything of significance in life, there will be someone who opposes our progress. We must learn the delicate balance of being open to correction from trusted sources while remaining steadfast in moving forward with God's mission in spite of opposition. (Day 5)

   • When have you felt God directing you to a new opportunity? (page 164)

- What opposition did you encounter, and how did you handle it? (page 164)
- What would you do differently if you had it to do over? (page 164)

11. Think about all of your study and reflection this week.

- What thoughts or discoveries are sticking with you from this week's study?

Deeper Conversation (15 minutes)

Divide into smaller groups of two or three for deeper conversation. (Encourage the women to break into different groups each week.) Before the session, write on a markerboard or chart paper the question or questions you want the groups to discuss:

- Look back to the Scriptures and Questions from Day 4 on pages 157-158. Reflect on some criticism that you have received and judge it against the Scriptures and questions. Decide together with your group if it is helpful or hurtful criticism. (Spend about 5–7 minutes each, depending on how many are in your group.)

Give a two-minute warning before time is up so that the groups may wrap up their discussion.

Closing Prayer (5–10 minutes)

Close the session by taking personal prayer requests from group members and leading the group in prayer. Encourage members to participate in the Closing Prayer by praying out loud for one another and the requests given.

Week 6

Daniel

Thriving in Messy Circumstances
Daniel 1–3

Leader Prep

Bible Story and Theme Overview

This week our study centered around the life of Daniel, a young man who, through no fault of his own, found himself living in a foreign country as a prisoner of war. Daniel and his friends encountered many messy situations while living in Babylon. They could have become depressed and discouraged as they faced one difficulty after another, but with God's help they found ways to thrive in their environment and maintain their values.

Main Point

Sometimes life is messy, and at times the messes feel completely overwhelming. God does not promise to spare us difficulties, but He does promise to be with us through them. And that is enough!

Key Scriptures

[5]*The king assigned them a daily ration of food and wine from his own kitchens. They were to be trained for three years, and then they would enter the royal service....*

[8]*But Daniel was determined not to defile himself by eating the food and wine given to them by the king. He asked the chief of staff for permission not to eat these unacceptable foods.*

(Daniel 1:5, 8)

[16]*Daniel went at once to see the king and requested more time to tell the king what the dream meant.*
[17]*Then Daniel went home and told his friends Hananiah, Mishael, and Azariah what had happened.* [18]*He urged them to ask the God of heaven to show them his mercy by telling them the secret, so they would not be executed along with the other wise men of Babylon.* [19]*That night the secret was revealed to Daniel in a vision. Then Daniel praised the God of heaven.*

(Daniel 2:16-19)

[16]*Shadrach, Meshach, and Abednego replied, "O Nebuchadnezzar, we do not need to defend ourselves before you.* [17]*If we are thrown into the blazing furnace, the God whom we serve is able to save us. He will rescue us from your power, Your Majesty.* [18]*But even if he doesn't, ... we will never serve your gods."*

(Daniel 3:16-18)

But when Daniel learned that the law had been signed, he went home and knelt down as usual in his upstairs room, with its windows open toward Jerusalem.

(Daniel 6:10)

What You Will Need

- *Messy People* DVD and a DVD player
- markerboard or chart paper and markers
- stick-on name tags and markers (optional)
- iPod, smartphone, or tablet and portable speaker (optional)

Session Outline

Welcome and Opening Prayer (5–10 minutes, depending on session length)

To create a warm, welcoming environment as the women are gathering before the session begins, consider lighting one or more candles, providing coffee or other refreshments, and/or playing worship music. (Bring an iPod, smartphone, or tablet and a portable speaker if desired.) Be sure to provide name tags if the women do not know one another or you have new participants in your group. Then, when you are ready to begin, pray the following prayer or offer your own:

Dear God, thank You for this journey through messiness. Thank You for showing us over and over how You love and restore messy people and relationships. Give us insight as we explore the story of Daniel and apply Your Word to our lives. Amen.

Icebreaker (5 minutes)

Invite the women to share short, "popcorn" responses to the following question:

- Where do you experience God's presence most powerfully?

Video (15 minutes)

Play the Week 6 video segment on the DVD. Invite participants to complete the Video Viewer Guide for Week 6 in the participant workbook as they watch. (page 200)

Group Discussion (25–40 minutes, depending on session length)

Note: More material is provided than you will have time to include. Before the session, select what you want to cover, putting a check mark beside it in your book. Page references are provided for questions related to questions or activities in the participant workbook. For these questions, invite participants to share the answers they wrote in their books.

Video Discussion Questions

- What happens when we just deal with surface issues in our lives and don't dig deeper? How can we do the hard work of getting rid of the real mess?
- What are some ways that Daniel demonstrated wisdom, humility, and courage throughout his life?
- What does it mean to insulate yourself from sin but not isolate yourself from others? How do we do this?
- How does knowing that Jesus is with us and for us and that He has overcome the world give you peace when trouble comes your way?
- How does remembering that Jesus wins help you to be brave and courageous so that you can live your very best life in Christ?

Participant Workbook Discussion Questions

1. Our lives are going to have messy, painful times. Sometimes they are the direct result of our own poor choices—a poorly chosen word, a bad decision, or an unhealthy lifestyle. But other times life becomes

painful through no fault of our own. Either way the question is, Will we thrive in our messy circumstances as Daniel did? (Day 1)

- Talk through the highlights of Daniel's story together. What were some of the messy situations he faced?
- Read Daniel 1:5, 8. What were they given to eat and drink, and what was Daniel's response? (page 172) How did Daniel demonstrate discipline as he navigated his messy situation?
- How does discipline help us when we aren't in control of our situation?

2. When faced with something that would force him to compromise his values in order to conform, Daniel resolved not to do it. He was not abrasive in how he handled the situation but humbly found a way to be true to God without offending those in authority. He was a young man of deep integrity and humility who displayed wisdom far beyond his years. And as a result of Daniel's discipline, he and his faithful friends were rewarded in the end. (Day 1)

- Read Romans 12:2 and Exodus 23:2. What do these verses urge us not to do? (page 173)
- When and how have you been swayed by the crowd in the past? When have you taken a stand against culture, and how has it affected your life? (page 173)
- As Christians living in our culture today, how can we relate to Daniel's situation in Babylon? (page 173)
- What are some challenges we face as individuals and as the church in not conforming to the values of this world? (page 173)

3. Pride is very hard to see in ourselves. Though others can easily see it, the mirror rarely reflects it accurately for us. In fact, pride often can be deceptive, showing up as stubbornness, arrogance, criticism, or competition. And it can be dangerous. (Day 2)

- Read Proverbs 16:18. What does pride destroy? (page 177)
- Read 1 Peter 3:8. What character qualities does this verse encourage? (page 177)
- Why is humility necessary if we are to live in harmony— demonstrating sympathy, love, and compassion? (page 177)

4. In Daniel 2 we see that Daniel's humility (plus a little wisdom and courage) not only saved his life and the lives of many others but also pointed the king of a pagan nation to the God of Israel. Daniel is a good example of a humble spirit before God and others; but when it comes to humility, Jesus is the best example. (Day 2)

   - Read Daniel 2:47. What did the king declare? How was Daniel's humility integral to the king's realization? (page 181)
   - Read Philippians 2:3-5. According to these verses, what does it mean to show the humility of Christ? (page 181)
   - What are some ways that our humility can point others to Christ? (page 181)

5. We may not be required to bow before a golden statue, but we must answer similar questions of integrity and conviction. We must continually choose whether to conform to the expectations of society or stand for God's principles. (Day 3)

   - Read Romans 12:2. In what situations have you found yourself pressured to conform? (page 185)
   - Is there a particular law or a rule that you find difficult to follow for reasons of integrity? If so, what is it, and what has been your response? (page 185)
   - What do Daniel and his friends show us about integrity?

6. As we face our own fiery furnaces, we will have the opportunity to stand or to fold. Like Shadrach, Meshach, and Abednego, may we have the strength to stand even when the outcome is unclear. Because in those painful moments, we can know with confidence that God will be with us. (Day 3)

   - Read Isaiah 43:2. What is God's promise to us? (page 187)
   - How does the promise of God's presence give you courage to face fiery trials?
   - What are some "fires" that you are facing today? How have you felt God's presence with you?

7. Wisdom is seeing things from God's perspective and responding in ways that please Him. But just knowing what we should do is not

enough. We have to put it into action. Daniel did both, even when it was scary. Wisdom is truth lived out, which spares us from pain and brings us blessings. (Day 4)

- According to Proverbs 2:6-7a, what is the source of wisdom? (page 190)
- Read James 3:13-17. What are the benefits of living wisely? (page 192)
- How have you seen people search for truth in ways other than turning to God? (page 192)

8. I don't know many people who would say that they don't want wisdom. Many of us like the idea of living by God's truths—until we find a truth that we don't like. It happens all the time. We want God's blessings, but we don't want to live according to all of God's standards. (Day 4)

- Is it possible to live according to God's Word and yet be disobedient to its truths? Explain your response. (page 193)
- What are some examples of common areas where people prefer their own wisdom over God's wisdom?
- In what areas and/or situations do you need to abandon your view and embrace God's wisdom? (page 193)

9. Even though the penalty of praying to anyone other than the king was death in a pit of lions, Daniel did not waver in his practices of honoring God. In fact, he did not even attempt to hide his prayers, choosing to pray in his upstairs room with the windows open. Daniel courageously and faithfully maintained his values. (Day 5)

- Has there been a time when you found it difficult to boldly practice your faith in the face of trials, challenges, or persecution for your beliefs or practices as a Christian? If so, describe it briefly. (page 196)
- Read 1 Peter 4:12. How would you restate this verse in your own words? (page 197)
- What are some examples of fiery trials that we face?

10. Daniel was able to stand strong because he knelt often. Daniel's practice of honoring God in his life gave him the courage to face whatever came his way; and in so doing, he proved to be a testimony

to others, including the king. Throughout his life, Daniel lived with an eternal perspective despite his temporary difficulties. This is an advanced maneuver but one that will serve us all well as we face the challenges of our own lives. (Day 5)

- How might this story have been different if Daniel had been too afraid to continue his prayer habit? (page 198)
- How might your faith and courage impact those around you? (page 198)
- What does it mean to live with an eternal perspective despite our temporary difficulties?

11. Think about all of your study and reflection this week.

- What thoughts or discoveries are sticking with you from this week's study?

Deeper Conversation (15 minutes)

Divide into smaller groups of two or three for deeper conversation. (Encourage the women to break into different groups each week.) Before the session, write on a markerboard or chart paper the question or questions you want the groups to discuss:

- Read Daniel 3:1-6, and describe the statue that King Nebuchadnezzar had built. Who was to bow down and worship the statue? What would be the signal for them to do this, and what would happen to those who refused? (page 184)
- What are some modern-day idols that we worship without even recognizing it?
- What do Daniel and his friends teach us about courage and integrity in our walk with God?

Give a two-minute warning before time is up so that the groups may wrap up their discussion.

Closing Prayer (5–10 minutes)

Close the session by taking personal prayer requests from group members and leading the group in prayer. Encourage members to participate in the Closing Prayer by praying out loud for one another and the requests given.

Video Viewer Guide: Answers

Week 1
need

centered

godly people

future

Week 2
first move

stuff

carefully

kindly

reconciliation /
resolution

Week 3
procrastinate

victim

temptation

control

Week 4
decide / respond

courage / new ways

changed / partner

Week 5
carefully

cool

information

what you can

Pray

Week 6
insulated

show up

faith / holiness

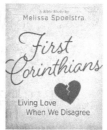

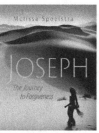
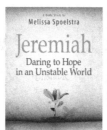

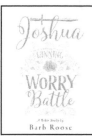
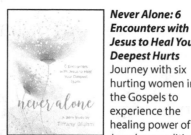
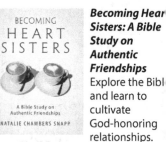

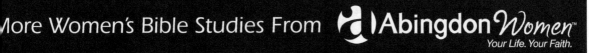

The Miracles of Jesus: Finding God in Desperate Moments
Invite God to work powerfully in your life.

Workbook ISBN:
9781501835452

Set Apart: Holy Habits of Prophets and Kings
Draw closer to God through spiritual practices.

Workbook ISBN:
9781426778421

Anonymous: Discovering the Somebody You Are to God
Discover your significance to Christ by exploring some of the "anonymous" women of the Bible.

Workbook ISBN:
9781426792120

Broken and Blessed: How God Used One Imperfect Family to Change the World
See how God brings blessings from our brokenness.

Workbook ISBN:
9781426778377

Namesake: When God Rewrites Your Story
Discover people in Scripture whose lives and names were changed forever by God.

Workbook ISBN:
9781426761874

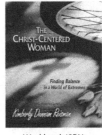

The Christ-Centered Woman: Finding Balance in a World of Extremes
Find balance and explore what the Bible teaches about Christ-centered living.

Workbook ISBN:
9781426773693

Embraced By God: Seven Promises for Every Woman
Explore the transformational power of God's love and acceptance.

Workbook ISBN:
9781426754418

This I Know for Sure
Learn to live a life of unshakable faith and leave a spiritual legacy.

Workbook ISBN:
9781426772450

A Woman's Place
Study a biblical look at vocation in the office, the home, in ministry, and beyond.

Participant Guide ISBN:
9781501849008

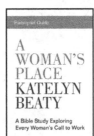

Coming September 2019 from Jennifer Cowart

Fierce: Lesser-Known Women of the Bible Who Changed the World
Discover how to be a fierce woman of God by living with courage, faith, and obedience.

Workbook ISBN: 9781501882906

CPSIA information can be obtained
at www.ICGtesting.com
Printed in the USA
LVHW101025310821
696115LV00010B/1

9 781501 863141